spot

BABY FARM ANIMALS

FOALS

by Anastasia Suen

AMICUS | AMICUS INK

ears

mane

Look for these
words and pictures
as you read.

hoof

legs

Have you ever seen a foal?
A foal is a baby horse.

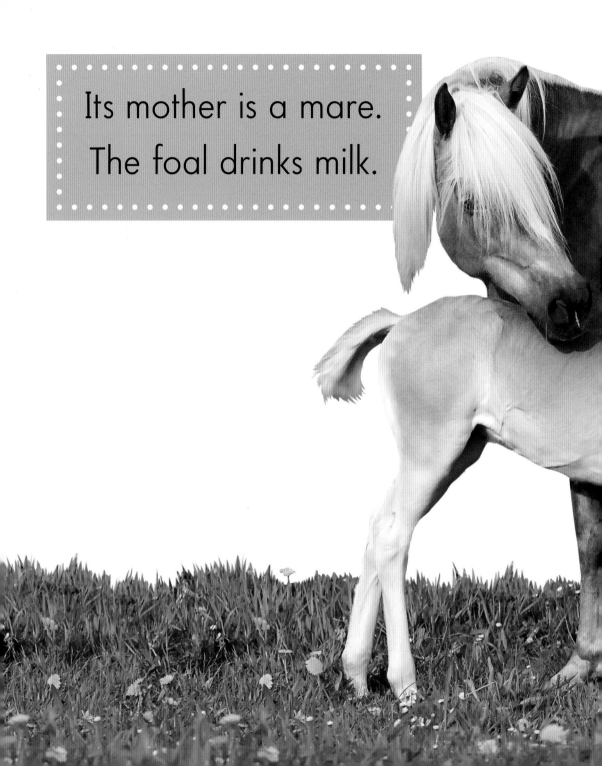

Its mother is a mare.

The foal drinks milk.

legs

Look at the foal's legs.
They are long.
. The foal walks two
hours after being born.

ears

Look at the foal's ears.
They are soft.
They turn to listen.

mane

Look at the foal's mane.
It sticks up.
It will grow long.

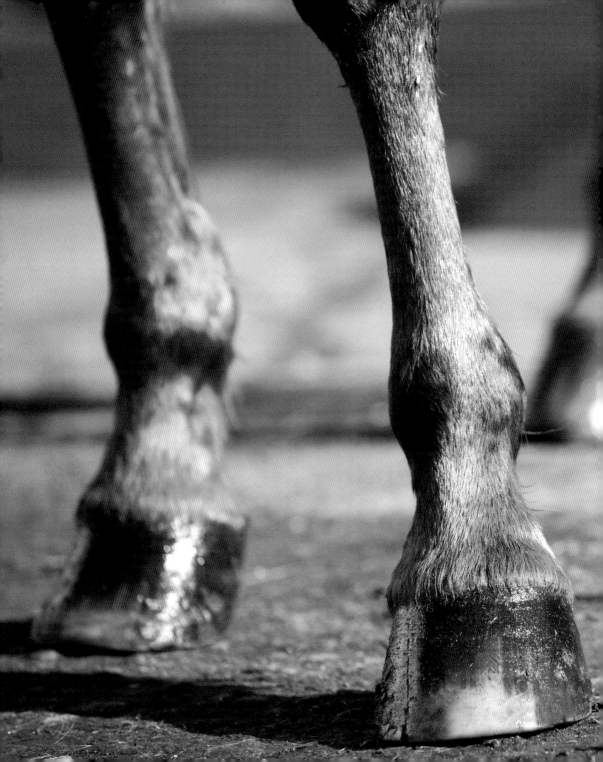

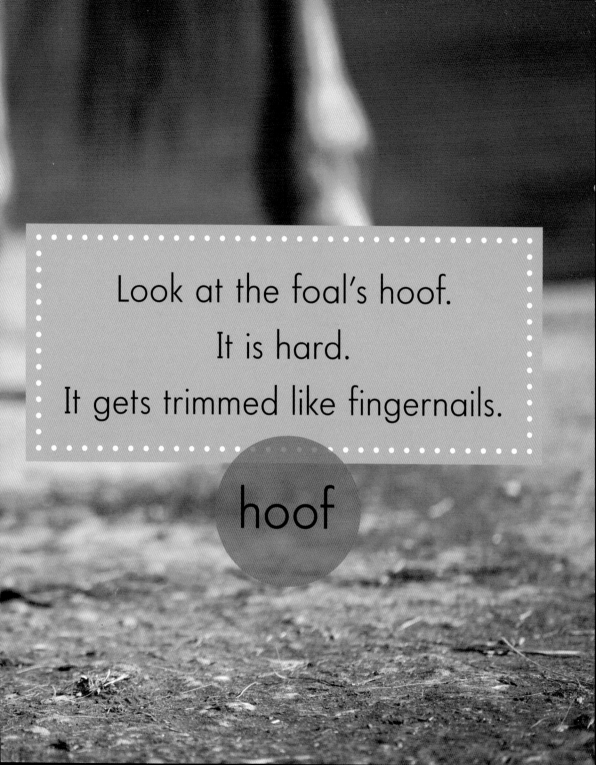

Look at the foal's hoof.
It is hard.
It gets trimmed like fingernails.

hoof

A foal stays with other horses.
She is part of a herd.
The herd runs.

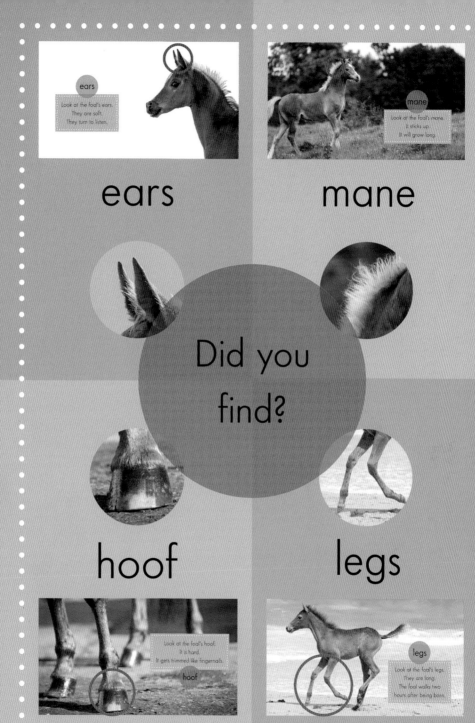

ears

mane

Did you find?

hoof

legs

Spot is published by Amicus and Amicus Ink
P.O. Box 1329, Mankato, MN 56002
www.amicuspublishing.us

Library of Congress Cataloging-in-Publication Data
Names: Suen, Anastasia, author.
Title: Foals / by Anastasia Suen.
Description: Mankato, MN : Amicus, [2019] | Series: Spot.
 Baby farm animals
Identifiers: LCCN 2017046899 (print) | LCCN 2017049596
(ebook) | ISBN 9781681515694 (pdf) | ISBN 9781681515311
(library binding) | ISBN 9781681523699 (pbk.)
Subjects: LCSH: Foals--Juvenile literature.
 Classification: LCC SF302 (ebook) | LCC SF302 .S84 2019
(print) | DDC 636.1--dc23
LC record available at https://lccn.loc.gov/2017046899

Printed in China

HC 10 9 8 7 6 5 4 3 2 1
PB 10 9 8 7 6 5 4 3 2 1

Wendy Dieker and
 Mary Ellen Klukow, editors
Deb Miner, series designer
Aubrey Harper, book designer
Holly Young, photo researcher

Photos by iStock/Kerrick cover,
GlobalP 1, Zuzule 3, castenoid
10–11, edenexposed 12–13,
a_Taiga 14; Shutterstock/Katho
Menden 4–5; Age Fotostock/
Juniors Bildarchive 6–7; Alamy/C.
Slawik/Juniors 8–9

FOALS